10/14

# DOWNSIDE
## OF DRUGS

# Methamphetamine and Other Amphetamines

# DOWNSIDE OF DRUGS

# DOWNSIDE OF DRUGS

# Methamphetamine and Other Amphetamines

## Rosa Waters

Mason Crest

Mason Crest
450 Parkway Drive, Suite D
Broomall, PA 19008
www.masoncrest.com

Printed and bound in the United States of America.

First printing
9 8 7 6 5 4 3 2 1

Series ISBN: 978-1-4222-3015-2
ISBN: 978-1-4222-3023-7
ebook ISBN: 978-1-4222-8809-2

Cataloging-in-Publication Data on file with the Library of Congress.

# Contents

# INTRODUCTION

One of the best parts of getting older is the opportunity to make your own choices. As your parents give you more space and you spend more time with friends than family, you are called upon to make more decisions for yourself. Many important decisions that present themselves in the teen years may change your life. The people with whom you are friendly, how much effort you put into school and other activities, and what kinds of experiences you choose for yourself all affect the person you will become as you emerge from being a child into becoming a young adult.

One of the most important decisions you will make is whether or not you use substances like alcohol, marijuana, crystal meth, and cocaine. Even using prescription medicines incorrectly or relying on caffeine to get through your daily life can shape your life today and your future tomorrow. These decisions can impact all the other decisions you make. If you decide to say yes to drug abuse, the impact on your life is usually not a good one!

One suggestion I make to many of my patients is this: think about how you will respond to an offer to use drugs before it happens. In the heat of the moment, particularly if you're feeling some peer pressure, it can be hard to think clearly—so be prepared ahead of time. Thinking about why you don't want to use drugs and how you'll respond if you are asked to use them can make it easier to make a healthy decision when the time comes. Just like practicing a sport makes it easier to play in a big game, having thought about why drugs aren't a good fit for you and exactly what you might say to avoid them can give you the "practice" you need to do what's best for you. It can make a tough situation simpler once it arises.

In addition, talk about drugs with your parents or a trusted adult. This will both give you support and help you clarify your thinking. The decision is still yours to make, but adults can be a good resource. Take advantage of the information and help they can offer you.

Sometimes, young people fall into abusing drugs without really thinking about it ahead of time. It can sometimes be hard to recognize when you're making a decision that might hurt you. You might be with a friend or acquaintance in a situation that feels comfortable. There may be things in your life that are hard, and it could seem like using drugs might make them easier. It's also natural to be curious about new experiences. However, by not making a decision ahead of time, you may be actually making a decision without realizing it, one that will limit your choices in the future.

When someone offers you drugs, there is no flashing sign that says, "Hey, think about what you're doing!" Making a good decision may be harder because the "fun" part happens immediately while the downside—the damage to your brain and the rest of your body—may not be obvious right away. One of the biggest downsides of drugs is that they have long-term effects on your life. They could reduce your educational, career, and relationship opportunities. Drug use often leaves users with more problems than when they started.

Whenever you make a decision, it's important to know all the facts. When it comes to drugs, you'll need answers to questions like these: How do different drugs work? Is there any "safe" way to use drugs? How will drugs hurt my body and my brain? If I don't notice any bad effects right away, does that mean these drugs are safe? Are these drugs addictive? What are the legal consequences of using drugs? This book discusses these questions and helps give you the facts to make good decisions.

Reading this book is a great way to start, but if you still have questions, keep looking for the answers. There is a lot of information on the Internet, but not all of it is reliable. At the back of this book, you'll find a list of more books and good websites for finding out more about this drug. A good website is teens.drugabuse.gov, a site compiled for teens by the National Institute on Drug Abuse (NIDA). This is a reputable federal government agency that researches substance use and how to prevent it. This website does a good job looking at a lot of data and consolidating it into easy-to-understand messages.

What if you are worried you already have a problem with drugs? If that's the case, the best thing to do is talk to your doctor or another trusted adult to help figure out what to do next. They can help you find a place to get treatment.

Drugs have a downside—but as a young adult, you have the power to make decisions for yourself about what's best for you. Use your power wisely!

—*Joshua Borus, MD*

# 1. WHAT ARE AMPHETAMINES?

All drugs are chemicals that in some way change the way the body works. Some drugs make the body work faster than normal. This type of drugs are known as stimulants. Other types of drugs slow down the body, and these drugs are called depressants. Other types of drugs change how the body acts in other ways. Some drugs fight diseases. Amphetamines are a kind of drugs that stimulate the *central nervous system*, producing an increase in alertness and wakefulness, as well as a state of excitement.

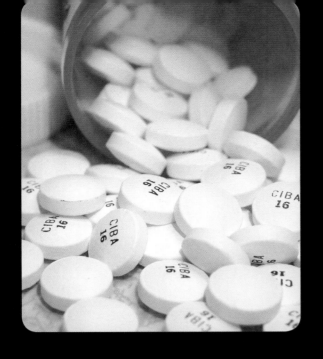

Amphetamines were originally created to be medicines. They were used to treat asthma and nasal congestion, sleep disorders, and *hyperactivity*.

Drugs can help human beings live healthier lives. We think of these types of drugs as medicines. But drugs can also be dangerous when they're not taken in the way they were intended to be used. Even legal, helpful drugs can be deadly when they're not taken in the ways they are supposed to be used. When amphetamines are abused, they can be very dangerous.

# 2. WHAT IS METHAMPHETAMINE?

Methamphetamine (often known as meth or crystal meth) is one kind of amphetamine. Like all amphetamines, it is a stimulant. It speeds up the processes of the central nervous system. But it is even stronger than most other amphetamines, which makes it even more dangerous.

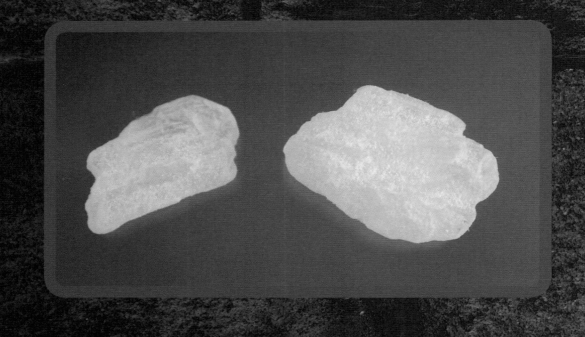

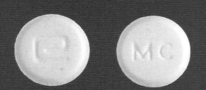

There is one form of legal methamphetamine, which is used to treat obesity and attention-deficit hyperactivity disorder (ADHD)—but usually meth is a street drug that is created only for the purpose of getting people high. Street meth doesn't have any medicinal uses.

As shown on the popular TV show *Breaking Bad*, meth has to be "cooked" in a lab.

The waste from meth labs is extremely hazardous. Common meth lab waste includes various chemicals, soda bottles, kitty litter, lithium batteries, ether, matches, and pill packaging.

Other street names for meth:

- speed
- chalk
- crank
- ice
- crystal
- glass

# 3. WHAT IS THE DOWNSIDE OF THESE DRUGS?

Amphetamines can be very addictive. This means that people can come to depend on them. They may feel as though they can't get through their lives without taking more and more of these drugs. Their bodies may truly need these drugs in order to function normally.

Drug addiction is like a hook. Once a person is caught on this hook, it's not easy to escape!

2005© "Faces of Meth"

2.5 Years Later

When people are addicted to a drug, they feel physically sick if they don't take that drug. The drug is more than a habit. When people are addicted, they no longer have control over their lives. They may stop hanging out with their friends. They may fail to live up to their responsibilities at school and work. Nothing seems interesting to them except getting more of their drug. Nothing else seems important. If their addiction goes on long enough, they may lose their friends. They may flunk out of school and lose their jobs.

The woman in this image is addicted to meth. The picture on the left shows how she looked when she started out. The picture on the right shows what she looked like after two and a half years of addiction to meth. Her addiction turned her into an old woman.

# 4. WHAT DO AMPHETAMINES LOOK LIKE?

Amphetamines come in many shapes, colors, and sizes. Legal amphetamines are often sold as tablets, like those shown here, or as capsules. When they're sold illegally, however, they may be crushed into a powder and packaged in aluminum foil, plastic bags, or small balloons.

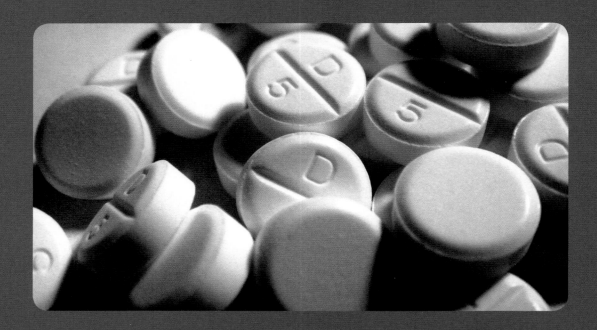

Amphetamine powder can range in color from white to brown. Sometimes it can be orange or dark purple. It has a strong smell and bitter taste.

# WHAT DOES METH LOOK LIKE?

Methamphetamine looks like crystals, but it can also be sold as a powder.

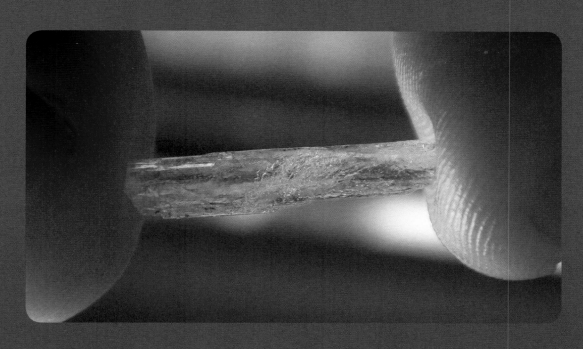

# 5. HOW ARE AMPHETAMINES USED?

Amphetamines are usually swallowed in pill form—but when they're ground up into powder they can be smoked. The powder can be also mixed with a liquid and injected with a needle into a user's bloodstream.

Some people snort powdered amphetamines with a straw up into their noses, where it is absorbed into the blood through the thin skin inside the nose.

# HOW IS METH USED?

Powdered meth is used in the same way other amphetamines are. Crystal meth, however, is usually smoked in a glass pipe, like the one shown here.

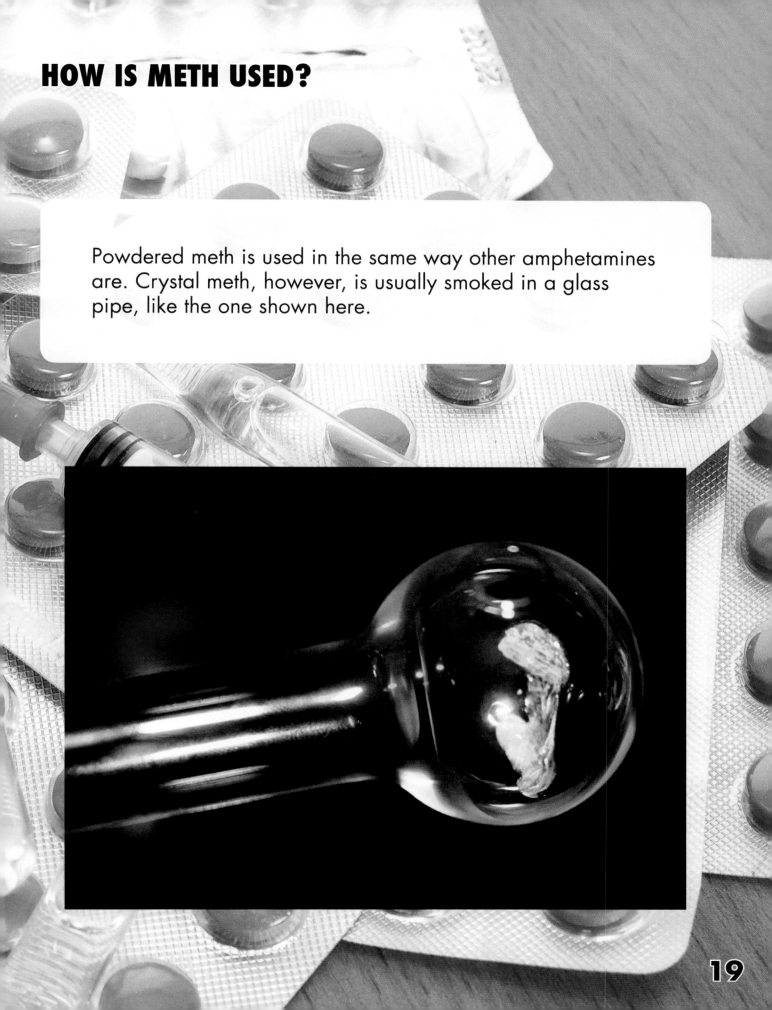

# 6. WHAT DO AMPHETAMINES DO TO YOUR BODY?

Amphetamines are powerful chemicals that affect your body in both short-term and long-term ways.

Short-term effects of amphetamines:

- increased heart rate
- reduced appetite
- increased energy
- increased blood pressure
- *dilation* of the pupils

Long-term use of amphetamines can cause:

- *insomnia* and restlessness
- trembling
- death
- weight loss
- *strokes*

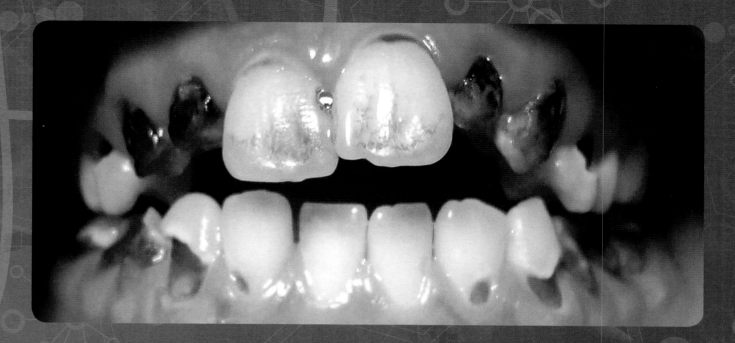

Using meth can cause dental problems, including rotting teeth and gum disease. It can make your mouth look like this.

Meth use drastically changes people's appearance. The image on the left shows how this woman looked before she became addicted to meth. The image on the right shows how she looked a year and a half later.

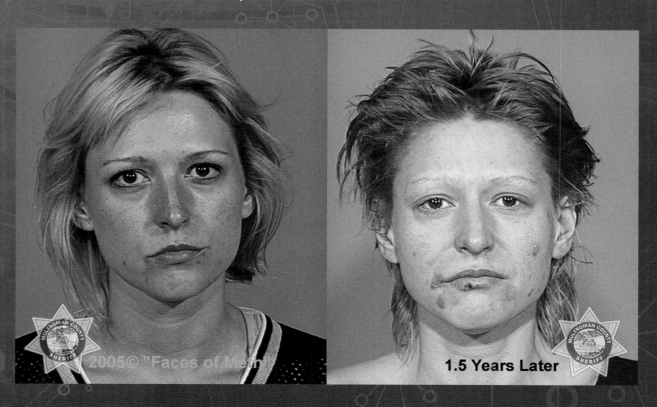

1.5 Years Later

# 7. WHAT DO AMPHETAMINES DO TO YOUR BRAIN?

Inside your brain are nerve cells, called neurons. Your emotions, your movements, your thoughts, and all your body functions depend on messages being passed between your neurons, like electricity traveling through a wire. However, there are tiny spaces between nerve cells, called synapses. Your neurons need chemicals called neurotransmitters to carry the messages across these spaces. Two kinds of neurotransmitters are dopamine, which is related to feelings of pleasure, and norepinephrine, which is connected to feelings of excitement and anxiety. Your body normally produces these chemicals.

If you take amphetamines, it makes your body produce more dopamine and norepinephrine than usual. When your brain is flooded with these neurotransmitters, you'll feel a "rush." But if you keep using amphetamines, that good feeling can become something pretty scary. Extended meth use is especially dangerous.

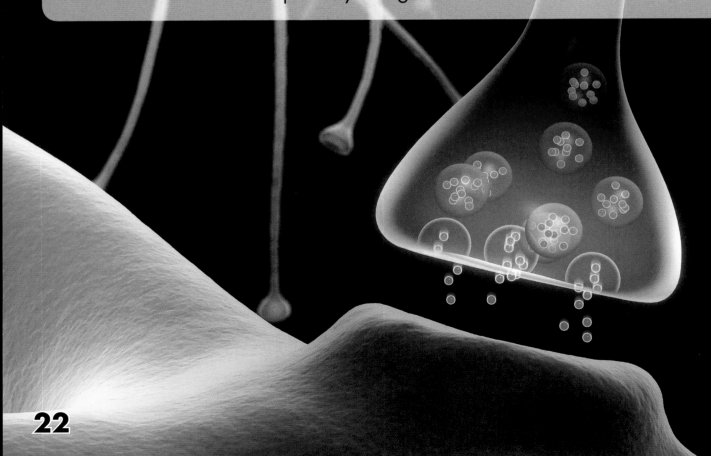

In some cases, meth users stop eating and sleeping. They take more meth every few hours for days, "binging" until they either run out of the drug or become too messed up to continue. Long-term meth use can make people feel scared all the time. It can give them *hallucinations*. It can make them engage in *repetitive* behaviors—like washing their hands again and again, vacuuming their floors without being able to stop, or taking a machine apart and putting it back together over and over. They may believe that they have bugs crawling under their skin—and then they can scratch until they bleed, trying to get rid of the imaginary insects. They may become violent. They may become *psychotic*.

A chemist in Romania created the first amphetamine back in 1887. He used a Chinese plant called ma-haunge to create a new chemical. More than thirty years later, doctors came up with a use for the new chemical when they noticed that it dilated and cleared congestion from breathing passages. In 1932, amphetamines were put into the Benzedrine Inhaler and sold as over-the-counter medicine for people suffering from colds, allergies, and asthma.

The drug became popular very quickly— but within a few years, young adults looking for a cheap high started taking the amphetamine strips out of Benzedrine Inhalers and putting them into cups of coffee. Some teens just chewed up the strips and swallowed them. Either way, the amphetamine gave them an intense rush.

Meanwhile, by 1937, doctors were also using amphetamine tablets to treat depression. People also noticed that taking amphetamine pills was a good way to keep from getting sleepy—and by World War II, lots of people, including soldiers, truck drivers, students, athletes, and housewives, were taking the drug to help them stay alert after long days and nights of work. The drug was also sold as a weight-loss pill.

Finally, in 1965, people realized that the potential for amphetamine abuse was just too great. In the United States, the Food and Drug Administration (FDA) removed many over-the-counter forms of amphetamine. The dangers of this drug had proved to be far greater than any of its benefits.

A 1944 advertisement for the Benzedrine Inhaler:

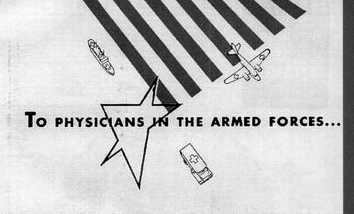

**Benzedrine Inhaler is available to High Altitude Flying Personnel!**

Benzedrine Inhaler is now an official item of issue in the Army Air Forces.

It is available to Flight Surgeons for distribution to high altitude flying personnel, for relief of nasal congestion.

**Benzedrine Inhaler**

A Volatile Vasoconstrictor . . . Outstandingly Convenient, But, First and Foremost, A Highly Effective Therapeutic Agent.

Each Benzedrine Inhaler contains racemic amphetamine, S.K.F. 250 mg.; oil of lavender, 75 mg.; and menthol, 12.5 mg.

SMITH, KLINE & FRENCH LABORATORIES · PHILADELPHIA

**To physicians in the armed forces...**

All last winter physicians in the Armed Forces kept writing us for their "usual" BENZEDRINE INHALERS. ★ Evidently, under Service conditions—the most exacting test of practical usefulness—Benzedrine Inhaler demonstrated its unique combination of convenience and therapeutic effectiveness. ★ So we hope that any Army or Navy physician who wishes a Benzedrine Inhaler for his personal use, will return the coupon below or drop us a postcard. (We have no other way of obtaining your address.) ★ Smith, Kline & French Laboratories, 107 N. Fifth St., Philadelphia 5, Pa.

**BENZEDRINE INHALER**

A VOLATILE VASOCONSTRICTOR
*In the new plastic tube...*

# 9. ARE THERE LEGAL AMPHETAMINES?

Doctors still use amphetamines sometimes to treat medical conditions, including ADHD, *narcolepsy*, and obesity.

The following drugs are all legal amphetamines:

- dextroamphetamine
- levoamphetamine
- methylphenidate
- lisdexamfetamine

## ARE THEY LESS DANGEROUS THAN ILLEGAL AMPHETAMINES?

Legal amphetamines are equally as dangerous as street amphetamines. In fact, most amphetamines being sold on the streets are actually the same drugs that can also be *prescribed* legally by a doctor.

Even when taken as prescribed, legal amphetamines can lead to physical and psychological *dependence*. These drugs are very habit forming. Continued use of amphetamines, even legal amphetamines, can lead to addiction and mental disorders.

# 10. ARE THERE "NATURAL" AMPHETAMINES?

Ephedra is sometimes considered to be a "natural" form of amphetamine. Ephedra is another name for the Chinese plant ma-haunge, which is the main ingredient used to *synthesize* amphetamines. Ephedra has been sold as a natural "supplement" intended to increase athletic performance and aid in weight loss—but in 2004, the FDA banned the sale of all supplements containing ephedra. It is now illegal in the United States, and many international athletic organizations, including the Olympics, have banned its use.

# ARE THEY LESS DANGEROUS THAN OTHER AMPHETAMINES?

Ephedra is illegal because it proved to be deadly. People who took it to lose weight or gain energy sometimes died.

Don't make the mistake of thinking that "natural" drugs are safe! Just because something comes from a plant, doesn't mean it's not dangerous. Plants can contain chemicals that have powerful effects on the human body and brain. Think of all the plants that are poisonous: they're natural, but they're deadly!

amphetamines are dangerous and addictive, but meth is especially so. It can cause permanent brain damage, even after t one use. This may mean that users become depressed, findi e pleasure in life—and this feeling can last even after they've pped taking meth. This is because their brains can no longer ate dopamine, the neurotransmitter necessary for our brains rceive pleasure.

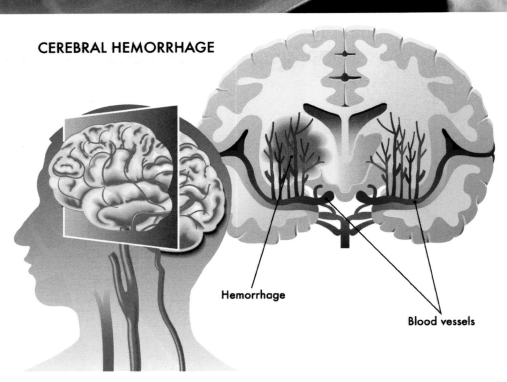

**CEREBRAL HEMORRHAGE**

Hemorrhage

Blood vessels

Meth brain damage can also be due to increased blood pressure, which can kill brain cells or cause strokes. When autopsies are done on meth users who have died, their brains often reveal that they've had thousands of small *hemorrhages*, called strokes. These mini-strokes cause *premature* aging. They can also cause premature senility. And they can cause death.

The photographs belowshow the way meth can turn a person who is fairly young into someone who looks sick and old. The image on the left shows a man before he started using meth—and the image on the right shows the same man just three months later. The average meth addict only lives five to seven years after becoming addicted.

2005© "Faces of Meth"    3 Months Later

# 12. DO TEENS USE METH AND OTHER AMPHETAMINES?

Researchers have found some good news about teenagers and amphetamines—a lot fewer teens are using these drugs today. The percentage of young adults trying amphetamines has gone down steadily since the 1990s, and fewer and fewer teens are using these drugs regularly.

A recent survey by CBS News revealed that 1 in 33 teens in the United States has tried meth, and a quarter of those surveyed said crystal meth was easy to get and "had some benefits." Even though use has decreased among teens, crystal meth is still one of the most widely used drugs among young people.

It's good news that fewer young adults are using amphetamines—but if 12 teens out of every 100 are using these drugs, as some research indicates, that's still too much, considering how dangerous amphetamines are.

# 13. HOW CAN YOU TELL IF SOMEONE IS BECOMING ADDICTED TO AMPHETAMINES?

One of the main symptoms of any kind of addiction is that the person continues to use the drug, even though it's hurting him physically, emotionally, and *socially*. He no longer has control of the drug—instead, the drug controls him.

Other signs of amphetamine addiction:

- heightened mood or *euphoria*
- suddenly increased sociability and self-confidence
- tolerance (The person needs to take more of the substance to achieve the desired effects.)
- rapid breathing
- dilated pupils
- increased energy
- decreased appetite
- increased body temperature
- overly talkative
- engaging in risky behaviors, such as dangerous sex, driving too fast, or other risk-taking
- failure to read *social cues*
- acting excited and silly
- difficulty with problem solving
- diminished interest in school, work, and social activities

# 14. ARE AMPHETAMINES AND CRIME CONNECTED?

Amphetamine abuse and crime go hand-in-hand. Meth is especially linked with crime: meth users commit between 50 and 70 percent of all property crimes in order to get money to buy their drugs. Meth production is also a major criminal activity. The map on this page shows where most of the illegal production is going on in the United States.

**Calendar Year 2012**
**Total: 11,210**

**Total of All Meth Clandestine Laboratory Incidents Including Labs, Dumpsites, Chem/Glass/Equipment**

Source: El Paso Intelligence Center (EPIC)National Seizure System (NSS)
Query Date January 27, 2013

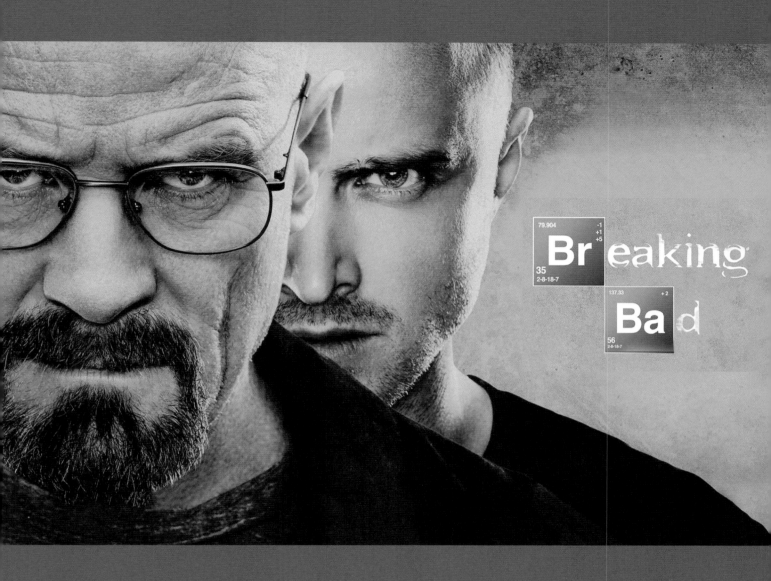

The TV show *Breaking Bad* revealed to viewers the connection between meth production, violence, and crime.

# WHAT HAPPENS IF YOU MIX ALCOHOL AND AMPHETAMINES?

The mixture of alcohol and amphetamines can be deadly.

Amphetamines are stimulants that drastically increase central nervous system activity, making the user feel excited and restless. Alcohol, however, is a depressant, which has the opposite effects on the body. When mixed together, the person may not be able to feel that she has had too much of either drug. This can lead to overdoses, which can cause *coma* or even death.

Some of the other health risks of mixing alcohol with amphetamines include:

- irregular heart rhythms
- intestinal problems such as nausea, vomiting, and diarrhea
- extreme *paranoia* and *psychosis*
- muscle spasms
- severe headaches
- kidney disease

# 16. MORE QUESTIONS?

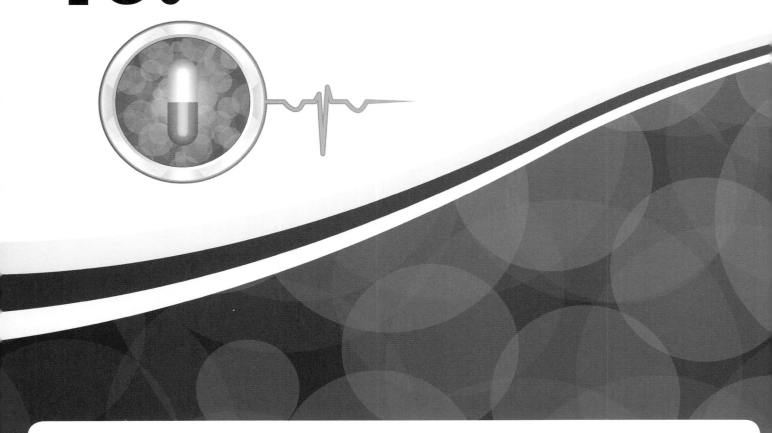

## What should I do if I think someone has overdosed on amphetamines?

An overdose is when someone takes too much of any drug or medication, so that it causes serious, harmful symptoms or even death. If you think you or someone else has overdosed on a drug, you should always call 911 immediately. If it's not an emergency but you have questions about preventing an overdose, you can also call the National Poison Control Center (1-800-222-1222) from anywhere in the United States. It is a free call and it's *confidential*. You can call for any reason, 24/7.

## Can I use amphetamines and stay safe?

If a doctor has prescribed an amphetamine to treat a medical attention that you have, you should be very careful to follow all your doctor's instructions for taking the drug. Never take a larger dose than what you were told to take, and never take your medication more often than the prescription tells you. If you follow your doctor's instructions exactly, letting her know any concerns you might have, you should be able to safely take this medication.

Street amphetamines are never safe, though. You can't know for sure how much of the drug you are getting in each dose, and you have no one to help you make sure you don't get addicted. Meth is especially dangerous. You cannot take meth and be safe!

# FURTHER READING

Anderson, Scott Thomas. *Shadow People: How Meth-Driven Crime Is Eating at the Heart of Rural America.* Folsom, Calif.: Coalition for Investigative Journalism, 2012.

Braswell, Sterling. *American Meth: A History of the Methamphetamine Epidemic in America.* Bloomington, Ind.: iUniverse, 2006.

Fletcher, Anne M. *Inside Rehab: The Surprising Truth About Addiction Treatment—and How to Get Help That Works.* New York: Viking, 2013.

Jensen, Taylor S. *Methamphetamine: Understanding Drugs and Addiction.* Saint Louis, Mo.: JK Publishing, 2012.

National Institute on Drug Abuse. *Methamphetamine: Abuse and Addiction.* Washington, D.C.: NIDA, 2012.

Rasmussen, Nicolas. *On Speed: The Many Lives of Amphetamine.* New York: NYU Press, 2008.

Sheff, David. *Clean: Overcoming Addiction and Ending America's Greatest Tragedy.* New York: Houghton Mifflin Harcourt, 2013.

Warburton, Lianne and Diana Califas. *Amphetamines and Other Stimulants.* New York: Chelsea House, 2007.

# FIND OUT MORE ON THE INTERNET

**Amphetamines**
amphetamines.com

**Drug Guide: Methamphetamine**
www.drugfree.org/drug-guide/methamphetamine

**Effects of Amphetamine Abuse**
www.narconon.org/drug-abuse/amphetamine-effects.html

**Important Facts About Amphetamine and Methamphetamine Abuse**
www.urmc.rochester.edu/encyclopedia/content.aspx?ContentTypeID=1&ContentID=1431

**Methamphetamine**
www.nlm.nih.gov/medlineplus/methamphetamine.html

**Meth Project**
www.methproject.org

**Office of National Drug Control Policy: Methamphetamine**
www.whitehouse.gov/ondcp/meth-intro

**Signs and Symptoms of Amphetamine Abuse**
www.narconon.org/drug-abuse/amphetamine-signs-symptoms.html

**The Truth About Crystal Meth**
www.drugfreeworld.org/drugfacts/crystalmeth.html

# GLOSSARY

*autopsies:* Medical examinations performed on dead bodies to find the cause of death.

*central nervous system:* Your brain and spinal cord, which work together to control your entire body.

*coma:* A deep unconsciousness that you can't wake up from.

*dependence:* A state of needing something to live or function correctly.

*dilation:* When something circular like your blood vessels or pupils gets larger.

*euphoria:* A feeling of intense happiness.

*hallucinations:* Things that you see and hear that aren't really there.

*hemorrhages:* Broken blood vessels; bleeds.

*hyperactivity:* Having an uncontrollable amount of energy.

*insomnia:* When you have trouble falling or staying asleep.

*narcolepsy:* A condition where you fall asleep at random times.

*paranoia:* A feeling of fear and distrust, without having a good reason to feel that way.

*premature:* Happening sooner than is normal.

*prescribed:* Told by a doctor that you need to take a certain drug.

*psychotic:* Insane.

*repetitive:* Done over and over.

*senility:* A state of having lost mental ability as you age.

*social cues:* Hints of how people feel given by the tone of their voices or their body language.

*socially:* Having to do with your relationships with other people.

*strokes:* Blocked or burst blood vessels in the brain, which can cause brain damage.

*synthesize:* Produce artificially.

# INDEX

# PICTURE CREDITS

# ABOUT THE AUTHOR
# AND THE CONSULTANT

**ROSA WATERS** lives in New York State. She has worked as a writer for several years, producing works on health, history, and other topics.

**DR. JOSHUA BORUS, MD, MPH,** graduated from the Harvard Medical School and the Harvard School of Public Health. He completed a residency in pediatrics and then served as chief resident at Floating Hospital for Children at Tufts Medical Center before completing a fellowship in Adolescent Medicine at Boston Children's Hospital. He is currently an attending physician in the Division of Adolescent and Young Adult Medicine at Boston Children's Hospital and an instructor of pediatrics at Harvard Medical School.